AF326560

FOLKLORE OF THE SHETLAND ISLES

BY

JOHN SPENCE

FOLK-LORE

FOLK-LORE

ARLY in the present century many superstitious beliefs and observances were common in Shetland which are now altogether forgotten, or only to be found lingering in some outlying districts. The old world ways of the Shetlanders have given place to a new order of things. Our domestic, social, and industrial life is conducted on different lines. Hence it is evident that even the remembrance of the times of our forefathers will pass away for ever with the present generation. It is hoped that this humble attempt to embalm on the

printed page these recollections of the past
will meet with the approbation of every
lover of the " Old Rock."

Of all classes, fishermen appear to have
been most superstitious. No doubt this
arose in a great measure from the nature
of their hazardous and precarious calling.
The ever fitful wind and changing sea, the
lottery of fish catching, the imminent peril
and hairbreadth escapes to which they
were exposed, fostered a belief in the
supernatural.

When a fisherman left his house to pro-
ceed to his boat, it was considered most
unlucky to call after him, even though he
had left something very essential behind;
and he was very particular as to meeting a
person by the way, lest they should have
an " evil eye " or an " ill fit." It was considered a good omen to meet an imbecile
or a person deformed from the birth.
These were called " Gude's pör," and were
suitable *aamas bairns*. After meeting one
of such, if the voyage had been at all pros-

perous, they were rewarded with an *aamas* or *kjoab*. The person who attempted to cross a fisherman's path when on his way to the boat, intended to do him scathe.

When such was really done, the fisherman, on coming to the point of crossing, took out his *skön* or *tullie* (sea knife), and made a scratch on the ground in the form of a cross, uttering (together with a spittle) the word *twee-te-see-dee*. The sign of the cross was considered an antidote against the intended evil, and the spittle an emphatic expression of contempt for the unchancy hag.

When a crew assembled at their boat at the beginning of the season, each man had his "ain lug o' da taft," or seat for pulling, and this order was never altered. If one had occasion to pass from one part of the boat to another, it was considered very unlucky to go between a man and his *kabe*. On leaving the land the boat was always turned with the sun—from east to west— never in the opposite direction, which was termed *widdershins.* The movements of witches were always made against the sun, and by whirling a wooden *cap* in water or a hand-mill on a bare *looder* (wooden bench-on which the mill rested), they were supposed to be able to raise the wind like Furies, and toss the sea in wild commotion capable of destroying anything afloat, from a cock boat to an armada. But to return to the fishermen. Their chief subject of conversation was the weather forecasts. The older and more experienced men would read the sky and explain the various appearances, and there is little doubt that from keen observation they were able to foretell the weather with considerable accuracy. They possessed a stock of weather lore of which we, in these days of barometers and storm-signals, know little.

The movements and conduct of certain birds and animals were looked upon as prognostics of the weather. For example, to hear crows crying after sunset foretold the coming day to be fair. The flight of the rain goose (the red-throated diver) was particularly noticed. When this bird was seen flying in an inland direction the weather was likely to be favourable, but when its flight was directed towards the sea the opposite was expected. Hence—

> " If the rain göse flees ta da hill,
>   Ye can geng ta da haf whin ye will;
>   Bit whin shö gengs ta da sea,
>   Ye maun draw up yir boats an flee."

Cocks crowing or the hens stirring abroad while rain is falling is a sign that it will soon be fair. Flocks of *snaa fowl* (snow bunting) seen before Winter Sunday (the last Sunday of October) foretell the approach of a severe winter.

A cat sitting with her back to the fire indicated cold weather, and washing her face with both the fore paws was a sure prognostic of coming rain; but when puss was observed sleeping on her *harns* (head turned down), fair weather might be expected.

When animals were observed rubbing themselves against stones or fences rain was supposed to be near, and the sensation that caused this behaviour in animals appears to have been felt in the human. An old fisherman might have been heard remarking : " Boys, he's gaein' ta be weet, for dey wir an oondömious yuk i' my head i' da moarnin'." A feeling of langour or tendency to sleep indicated the approach of thunder and rain—hence the saying : " It's fey folk that thunder waukens."

The various articles of furniture about a fisherman's house in the olden days were made from *raaga trees* (drift wood), and certain cracking sounds occasionally heard in such articles were considered sure indications of a change of weather. Sparks flying more than usual from a peat fire foretold the approach of frost ; and if *spunks* (sparks) were seen adhering to the bottom of the *maet* kettle when taken off the fire, snow was near if in winter, and cold, windy weather if in summer.

These terrestrial tokens were only secondary. The signs in the heavens above were the special study of the old *hafman*. On these he directed his anxious gaze as he plied the toilsome oar or hauled the fishing line. Halos round the sun or moon (called sun or moon *brochs*) were unwelcome sights, and were anxiously watched to see whether the sun did not "shine them out." It was observed that—

> " When the sun sets in a broch,
> He'll rise in a slauch;
> But if the broch dees awa
> E'er he sets i' da sea,
> He'll rise i' da moarnin'
> Wi' a clear e'e."

That is, if the halo disappears before sunset, the sun is likely to rise in a clear sky, and the following day will be fair. *Brynics* (what appears to be the end of a rainbow) seen on the horizon forbodes squally weather. Large masses of white clouds, called in winter *snaaie heads* and in summer *eestik heads*, were looked upon with ill favour, as they were sure either "ta rain aff or blaw aff." The *merry dancers* (aurora) extending to the zenith and unusually quick in their movements were considered an ill omen, but when they quietly displayed themselves in a graceful arch along the northern horizon the fishermen expected fair weather. The "carry" or motion of the clouds, with relation to the direction of the wind, was of special interest.

There was a notion that certain days of the week had to do with the weather. For example, a change for the better on Sunday was considered a favourable omen, but a bright Monday betokened a dark week. Wednesday's weather was true, and Friday was supposed to be either the best or the worst day in all the week.

There were certain times of the season when storms were specially expected. These were called *Rees*. There was *Buggle Ree*, about the 17th of March

(O.S.) ; *Paece Ree*, about Easter ; *Beltin Ree*, 20th May ; and the last three days of March, called the *Borrowing Days*, were generally expected to be boisterous. Most of these weather forecasts may be explained on natural and scientific grounds, but it is not the object of this work to do so.

I shall just mention one other means of foretelling the weather, which doubtless belongs to the Dark Ages of these islands. It is called the *milt token*, and is said to have been practised in some parts of Shetland. When the first *mert* was killed about Hallowmas, the milt or spleen of the animal was taken out and laid on a board, and six cuts were made crosswise, equidistant from each other. These cuts were not quite through the milt, the under side being left whole. They were named—the first, November ; the second, December ; the third, January ; and so on to April. The milt was now laid in a dark place for three days and three nights. It was then carefully examined, and if a cut had closed and presented a dry appearance, the month it represented was to be mild and dry; but if the cut was open and dry the month was supposed to be windy. An open and wet cut foretold wind and rain.

The Shetland fishermen had quite a vocabulary of old Norse words, which were generally used at sea, particularly when speaking of land objects; and it was deemed most unlucky to neglect the use of these expressions. No doubt the belief lingered that the ancient gods of the Norsemen still exercised power over the mysteries of the *jube* (the depths of the ocean), although their influence was waning before the light of the " White Christ." Hence it was considered prudent to use at least such words as had reference to the old faith. The following names were applicable to wind, etc., in its various degrees:

Gro or *Stö*—Wind in general.
Ungastö—Contrary wind.
Daggastö—Wet wind.
Guzzel—A dry, parching wind.

Pirr—Light airs in patches.
Laar—Light airs more diffused.
Stoor—A breeze.
Gooster—A strong breeze.
Gyndagooster—A storm.
Flan or *Tud*—A sudden squall.
Dachin—A lull.
Hain—To cease raining.
Runk—A break between showers.
Röd—Small rain.
Dagg—Wet fog.

The sea, like the wind, in its ever restless moods had various names applied to its movements. *Da mother di* was the name given to the undulations that roll landward even in calm weather, and by means of which the old *hafmen* could find his way in the thickest fog without the aid of a compass.

Di—A wave.
Söal—Swell occasioned by a breeze.
Töve—A short, cross, heavy sea.
Hak—Broken water.
Burrik—A sharp sea or " tide lump."
Bod—A heavy wave breaking on the shore.
Brim—Sound of sea breaking on the shore, especially when land could not be seen, as in a fog.

Brim-fooster—Sea breaking on a sunken rock or *baa*.
Faxin—A *baa* threatening to break.
Overskud or *Ootrug*—Broken or spent water or back-
wash.
Gruttik—Ebb tide.
Grimster—Ebb during spring tide.
Draag—The drift of a current.
Sokin or *Saagin*—Short period of still water between
tides.
Snaar—A turn or whirl in a current.
Roost—A rapid, flowing current, such as Sumburgh
Roost and Bluemull Roost.
Haf—The outer fishing ground.
Klak—Inshore fishing ground.
Skurr or *Klakaskurr*—Inshore fishing seat.
Fram—To seaward.

There were several names applied to the sea bottom, such as the *flör*, the *maar*, the *jube*, the *graef*, and the *ljoag*.

The old fishermen never spoke of things being lost or broken, and they never mentioned the *end* of anything. To be lost was expressed as having "gone to itself"; broken, "made up"; and the end was called the *damp*.

These were the chief terms applied to wind and sea, but of course they varied somewhat in different localities.   The boat also, and its furniture, together with land, animals, and other objects, were distinguished in the same quaint nomenclature, *e.g.*:

Faar—Boat.
Rae—Yard.
Stong—Mast.
Skegg—Sail.
Raemiks—Oars.
Bigg or *Bö*—House.
Frö or *Da Haimelt*—Wife.
Upstaander or *Baeniman*—Minister.
Yarmer or *Loader*—Precentor.
Fjandin—Devil.
Birtik—Fire.
Groitik—Meat-kettle.
Gludder or *Föger*—Sun.
Gloamer—Moon.
Boorik—Cow.
Nikker, Snegger, or *Soopaltie*—Horse.
Bjaener or *Hokner*—Dog.
Voaler, Vengie, Foodin, or *Krammer*—Cat.
Footik—Mouse.
Dryilla-skövie or *Dratsie*—Otter.
Flukner or *Klaager*—Hen.
Da Fish, Da Glyed Shield, or *Baldin*—Turbot.
Fjaedin—Whale.

Much valuable information regarding the significance and derivation of these and other old words used in Shetland may be found in Jakobsen's " Shetland Dialect and Place-Names."

The whale or *fjaedin*, or *bregdie* (as some of these aquatic monsters were called), was very much dreaded by the old fishermen, especially when one was seen alone. But they had means for protecting themselves against these dark denizens of the deep. This was simply an old copper coin. As soon as a whale was seen in close proximity to a boat, the copper penny was held in the water and scraped with a steel knife. It was believed that no whale would approach a boat so protected, and the fishermen soon had the pleasure of seeing their uncanny visitor give them a wide berth.

It was generally believed that steel instruments and silver coins possessed wonderful virtue in counteracting the malevolence of witches and *trows*. To cross witches above the breath, *i.e.*, on the forehead, so as to draw their *drörie* (blood) with a steel *noraleg* (a needle with the eye broken), deprived them of their power to hurt. A steel knife stuck in the mast of a boat was used as a means of raising the wind ; but some old fishermen would rather have rowed in a calm than had recourse to this expedient, which it was said had been the overthrow of some.

A story is told in verse by one of the Scotts of Lund of a belated traveller who was sorely pressed by a swarm of *hillfolk* or *trows* near the Heugins o' Watley :

> " Whin Johnnie cam' ta Watley burn,
>   They (*trows*) tried to dö 'im an ill turn ;
>   Bit haein his gun weel lod,
>   He cocked an' fired ta clear da rodd.
>   Bit Johnnie's gun refused ta fire,
>   Which made 'im cry : " O, dems er dier " ;
>   Then in the barrel he did drive
>   English shillings number five,
>   Which into bodies did divide
>   That walked close by Johnnie's side."

When instruments of domestic use or

weapons of warfare made of iron took the place of the old stone implements, their wonderful powers and superiority over the latter were no doubt attributed to magic. Hence the peculiar virtue of steel may be accounted for ; and the proverbial expression " as true as steel," when speaking of anything that is reliable or trustworthy. When an animal or even a person had died suddenly, they were supposed to be *elf-shot* ; and it was said that the elfin arrow was sometimes found : a minute, three-sided dagger of the finest steel.

THE HAF FISHING.

The old Shetland *sixern* or *haf* boat is now becoming obsolete. The great storm of 1881 appears to have given the death-blow to this time-honoured craft and to the old mode of fishing. The model is still preserved in the build of small boats, which in proportion to their size are the safest craft afloat.

About the beginning of the century they were modelled in Norway and temporarily put together there with *timmer pins*.   The pieces were numbered and shipped in

FIG. 10.—*Shetland Sixern.*

bundles to Shetland, where local carpenters were employed to "set them up," or put the parts together with *seam and röv*, and make them ready for sea.   In selecting a new boat, the service of an expert was commonly required to examine the *börds*, in order to detect the presence of *windy knots* or *wattery swirls* in the wood. The presence of these indicated that the boat was liable to *störa-brooken*, *i.e.*, blown up by the wind on land, or *misförn* at sea.

I was told by an old man that he called on a brother-fisherman to examine a boat that he had got built. After a careful overhaul of the newly built craft, he said : " Doo may hae a heavy haand, bit never a faerd haert. Watter 'ill no hurt dy boat, bit wind will. Tak' my wird, an' shord 'er weel." For ten long years this boat was used with safety and success, and every time she returned from sea was *yerd-fasted* in the winter *noost*. It came to pass, however, on a fair September night that they landed from the *piltik eela*, intending to make an early start for the ling *raiths*. As there were no signs of an impending storm, the boat was temporarily shored on the beach ; but before morning a sudden squall from the west had tossed the doomed craft to pieces among the rocks.

The old *haf* boat measured from 18 to 20 feet of keel, the stems bending outwards in a graceful curve, so as to give a length of some 26 feet over all. The breadth of beam was 6 to 7 feet, and the depth of hold 27 inches. The boat was divided into six compartments, viz., *fore-head, fore-room, mid-room, oost-room, shott, hurrik* or *kannie*. This last compartment next the stern was occupied by the steersman. The *shott* was double the size of a *room*, and formed a sort of hold in which the fish was carried. The various *rooms* were separated from each other by *fiska brods* (fish boards) ; and, in ordinary circumstances, a well-equipped boat had a place for everything and everything in its place. The sail, when not in use, was stowed in the fore-head, together with the buoys, buoy-ropes, and handline reels. The bread-box and *blaand* keg occupied the fore-room, while the ballast was placed in the mid-room, where the mast stood. The oost-room was always kept empty for the purpose—as its name implies—of *ousing* or discharging water.

Each man's share of *tows* or lines was termed a *packie*, and consisted of from 12 to 16 *bouchts* or hanks of lines, each measuring 40 fathoms. The hooks of wrought iron were *wupped* to *bidds* about four feet long, and placed along the ground line at a distance of nine yards apart. The fleet of lines carried was thus very considerable—extending to over four miles, and mounting 900 to 1000 hooks.

With reference to fishing hooks, it may be mentioned here that prior to the introduction of iron or steel hooks fish were caught by means of a small bit of hard wood or a splinter of bone from two to four inches long, attached to the end of the *tome* or *skoag*. This pin with the bait was held in position by a wrapping of coarse wool called *vaav*. When the fishermen "felt 'im" (became aware of a fish biting), he "gi'ed 'im da fadam," *i.e.*, he hauled in an arm's length of line with a sudden jerk.   The *vaaving* that held the *vaarnakle* or *berjoggel* (the wooden hook or rather pin) in an upright position now relaxed, and it turned horizontally across the mouth or throat of the fish, holding it fast while the fisherman gently drew it to the boat amidst profound silence, as it was deemed most unlucky to speak while a fish was being hauled.   Long after the introduction of the modern hook, fishermen still used *vaav* when fishing with very soft bait. Formerly sinkers were made of *klamal* or soap-stone, instead of lead as at present, and to this day fishermen speak of the *haandline stane* or *lead stane*, a remnant of the ancient practice.   Quite recently one of these ancient sinker stones was lifted on a fish hook at a *haf seat* off the north part of Unst.

These frail boats ventured a good distance from the land.   Rönies or Rönis

Hill (as Dr. Jakobsen prefers to spell it) in *skut*, or the Pobies *dippin'*, was by no means among the "crabs and *drooielines*," but signified a distance of thirty miles from the shore.

The fishermen were very particular to set their lines in a given straight course, indicated by *meiths* or marks on the land. This was chiefly to enable them the more readily to find the lines in the event of *making up* (breaking), and it was further considered that certain kinds of bottom kept fish more readily than others, and these patches of ground were known by names, sometimes that of the discoverer, as Maan's Raith, Tammas' Grund, Tirvil's Seat, etc.; but frequently they were distinguished by names having reference to their landmarks, as the Heug an' da Rimble, the Nippin Grund, the Vords, Hagmark an' da Röcok, etc. The fishing grounds nearest the land were called *klaks*, where handline fishing was practised, and were marked by cross *meiths*, so as to find the exact spot. These were called *klaka-skurrs*, and sometimes *seats*, and were named chiefly from their landmarks. Perhaps in some cases their names were indicative of the kind of bottom, as quite a number of these names ended in the suffix Mö, as Hoolnamö, Helyersmö, Fjelsmö, Tongamö, etc. Now, all these have soft or sandy bottoms, which may be implied in the particle Mö.

Outside the inshore fishing grounds, some five or six miles from land, were the *fram seats* or *raiths*, all marked and named as I have described. The usual fishing practised here was by handline, but the *haf* lines were also set during *aevaliss* (unsettled) weather.

Let us, gentle reader, imagine ourselves on board a *haf* boat. The crew have just completed the " setting " of the *tows*. The *bow* (buoy) is floating close at hand, attached to the boat by means of a *vaar-line*. Not a breath stirs the air, not a wave disturbs the bosom of the deep.

The ocean mirror reflects the many-tinted cloudlets sprinkled o'er the vault of heaven. The sun has set to us, and his golden rays have ceased to dance o'er the ripples; but Pobies' brow, still bathed in a flood of crimson light, sphinx-like rising from the waters, peers *framwards* like a sentinel of Night. No human being is in sight; a lazy-looking gull alone bears us company. Six weary hours of toil have passed since the crew had their last meal, and now they prepare to take supper. The skipper opens the *buggie* (a bag made of sheepskin), and takes out three *biddies* (very thick oatcakes), each of which he cuts in halves with his *sköne* (sea-knife). Handing a piece to each man, he expresses himself very reverently in the following terms: "Gude hadd Dy haand ower wis. Open da mooth o' da mamik (a ling having a roe), an' bring wis safe ta da kaavies (land)." Here was a prayer to God for preservation, guidance, and success, in a few syllables, more comprehensive and sincere than that uttered by the learned *upstaander* (minister). This humble meal of dry bread is washed down with a drink of *blaand* (a kind of whey made from buttermilk), after which the snuff-horn is passed round, and every man takes a pinch. It is noticeable that the crew in their conversation seldom give a negative reply. Instead of their saying " No," we hear *by-ye-blithe*.

It is now the *swaar o' dim* (midnight), and time to haul the *tows*. The east tide has *saaged* (ceased to flow), and the lines have got the *wast turnin'*. The distant hilltops are no longer visible. A thin veil of *ask* (haze) hangs o'er the horizon. We are now alone on the wide waste of waters. The gull that kept us company has gone to roost in the distant *maa-craig*. Nothing living can be seen save the occasional glint of a petrel footing the ripples.

Two of the crew, preparing to haul (or *hail*, as it is commonly pronounced), dress themselves in their leather *jubs* and *barm* skins. The man who hauls stands in the *oost-room*, face to *linebörd* (starboard); the other man sits astride the *shott* thwart. His work is to take in the fish, unhook and deposit them in the *shott*. His *sköne*, *huggie-staff* (fish-clip), and *kavel-tree* are at hand. He peers intently into the water as the line is being hauled. At length his hand seizes the *huggie-staff*, and knocking on the gunwale, he utters the word "Twee" (drawing the *ee* very long). This is no sooner said than he calls out "Wheeda"; and presently he exclaims: "Wheeda-hint-da-wheeda!" What does all this mean? It is glad tidings. The short prayer at supper-time has been answered—"da mooth o' da mamik" has been opened. It means that three ling are being hauled up hook after hook, and that the whole three are visible through the clear water to the eye of him that holds the *huggie-staff*.

Presently a smile of pleasure may be seen on the face of the man that hauls the line.   He feels a heavy weight and knows it to be the *nud o' a fish* (*i.e.*, a halibut, which is never named, but always spoken of as *da fish* or *da glyed shield*). Nothing comes more welcome to the gunwale of the *haf* boat.   It provided a valuable *nabert* (bait), and on its toothsome fish the crew feasted when on shore.   The *blugga-banes* of the halibut were stuck in the *waa o' da lodge* and under the *eft hinnie spot o' da sixern* for luck.   A large skate frequently formed part of the catch, and when deposited in the *shott* its formidable caudle appendage was a source of annoyance to the man in the *kavel*, until he took his *sköne* and *sneed aff her skövie* (cut off the tail).   The hauling of the lines in ordinary circumstances occupied from four to six hours.

It will be readily understood that these small boats, going to such a distance from the land and having such a length of lines to haul by hand, would be frequently overtaken by a storm, and ran the risk of being overwhelmed in making the wild headlands of Shetland. Though accidents did occur, yet it is matter for surprise that they were not more frequent. This was not so much owing to the sea-worthiness of the boats themselves, as to the skill and dexterity with which they were handled, In old times they never used the sail except they could "lie course." When a storm came off the land they manned the oars and *andowed* ahead ; and if the storm continued any length of time with severity, they ran the risk of being driven off and lost. But the most dangerous sailing, and that which required the most dexterous management, was running before the wind in a storm.

We shall again imagine ourselves on board a *haf* boat. The wind is blowing towards the land in angry gusts. The billows of the heavy ground swell toss their heads on high, and burst in angry roar. The waves chase each other in wild confusion. How frail does our craft appear! tossed like a chip midst the cease-less heave. The old skipper ships the rudder. God bless his weather-beaten face and nerve his hand to hold the helm. All he can do is to steer a straight course. Billows to right of him, billows to left of him, billows behind him, threaten to whelm him. But another also has a charge, and on him mainly does our safety depend. This is the man who holds the halyards (the *towman*), and has control of the sail.

When everything is ready the sail is hoisted, and the *towman* grasps the hal-yards. In one hand he holds the hoisting part and in the other the downhaul. Like a frightened steed the boat runs before the gale. Presently an angry wave comes rolling in our wake, and as it overtakes us we appear to be plunging headlong into the abyss of the waters; but the man who holds the halyards instantly lowers the sail a few feet so as to retard our motion. We seem for the moment to be hanging on a pivot of unstable water, but the wave passes on ahead and the sail is hoisted so as to accelerate our speed, and following close on the back of the spent sea, we run away from the succeeding wave. Meanwhile fish liver is being crushed in the *oost-room* and thrown on the troubled waters.

Sailing in a heavy sea, with the wind on the beam, the steersman has full control. He holds helm and sheet. This is also dangerous sailing, and requires expert management. The state of the sea along our path, both ahead and to windward, is carefully watched, and the boat is zig-zagged so that, if possible, breaking seas may be shunned ; but it often happens that an angry "lump" will toss itself in close proximity to our frail craft, so near that it may break aboard. But the man at the helm measures the wave with his eye, and if it threatens to strike the boat before the mast, the helm is put down and the sheet run off. The boat's head is thus brought towards the wave, which it vaults with the agility of a stag. But on the other hand, if the wave is likely to strike abaft the mast, the helm is put up with all speed, and the boat flees away from the angry wave, leaving it to spend its fury astern.

TROWS AND WITCHES.

About the middle of May the wives set their *kirns*, *milk-spans*, and *raemikles* (butter kits) in the *well stripe* to steep. The youngsters were employed to search for four-leaved *smora* (clover), the finding of which was considered extremely lucky, and anyone possessed of this holy plant was considered proof against the evil designs of witches.

Johnsmas was the season when witch-craft was most dreaded, and persons skilled in the black art deprived their neighbours of the profit of their milk and butter. Every housewife tried to keep her own, and used every precaution which seemed to her essential for this end.

Persons intent on witching a neighbour endeavoured to obtain the loan of some domestic utensil, especially about the time when a cow was expected to calve. But a wise woman would lend nothing at such a time, If a suspected person called, and even asked for a "drink o' *blaand*," the guidwife would seize a *lowin taand* (live coal), and chase the uncanny visitor out the door, throwing the fire after her, while she exclaimed : "Twee-tee-see-dee, du ill-vaum'd trooker!"

But it was difficult to preserve one's self from scathe, as the profit was supposed to be taken by such simple means as stepping over a cow's tether, plucking a handful of grass off the byre wall, or crossing a woman's path when on her way to milk the cows. Hence, in spite of every effort to prevent them, it often happened that witches carried out their dark designs at the expense of an artless neighbour.

When a person had good reason to believe that their cows had been witched, they commonly adopted such means as were considered most effectual in detecting the witch and bringing back the lost profit. This was sometimes a most elaborate affair, and required a considerable amount of nerve for its performance.

The following was related to me many years ago as having been done. A woman who suspected that her cows had been witched repaired to a march between two lairds' lands, and pulled fifteen green nettles by the roots. These were bound in a sheaf and placed on the *looder* of a water-mill.

Then the woman, providing herself with a triangular clipping of *skrootie claith*, two *noralegs*, a flint and steel, and a box of tinder, went to the mill at the hour of midnight, and taking the bundle of nettles, wended her way to the kirkyard of the parish. Arriving there, she went to the east side of the yard, and crossed the dyke back foremost.

Selecting an open space, the nettles are unloosed, and twelve of the number are placed end to end so as to form a circle. They are counted out backwards, while the following formula is slowly repeated :

" Da twal, da twal Apostles ;
Da 'leven, da 'leven Evangelists ;
Da ten, da ten Commandments ;
Da nine, da brazen shiners ;
Da eight, da holy waters ;
Da seven, da stars o' heaven ;
Da six, Creation's dawnin' ;
Da five, da timblers o' da bools ;
Da four, da gospel makers ;
Da tree, da triddle treevers ;
Da twa lily white boys that clothe themselves in green ;
Da een, da een dat walks alon', an' evermore sall rue."

Two of the remaining three nettles are now placed in the centre of the circle in the form of a St. Andrew's Cross. The two *noralegs* are also stuck into the *claith* in the form of a cross. Then with the *noralegs* in the one hand and the odd nettle in the other, she takes her stand within the sacred circle and exclaims :

> " With this green nettle
> And cross of metal
> I witches and wierds defy;
> O' warld's gear gi'e me nae mair
> Than the luck back ta da kye.
> Whae'er it be, else he or she,
> Dat's hurtit me an' mine,
> In sorrow may dey live an' dee,
> In pörta may dey pine.".

Then, suiting the action to the word, she sets fire to the tinder, saying : " So perish all my foes."

This wierd performance is now over, the nettles are collected, and the woman returns to her home in the small hours of the morning. The nettles are buried in the *gulgraave o' da vyeadie* (open drain) of the byre. The *noralegs* are stuck into the byre wall near the *vagil baand* of the cow, and as both rotted and corroded, so the witch was supposed to be seized with some wasting disease.

Trows or *hillfolk* were supposed to be

possessed of like passions as we are. They married and were given in marriage. They indulged their appetites in the good things of this life even as we do. They even required the services of the children of men for fiddlers, *howdies, gulyas*, and nurses, and there are alive to this day persons whose forebears were said to be so employed.

They, however, were not always friendly with men. They sometimes set covetous eyes on sheep and cattle, and on women and children. When they wished to take a nice *mert* (fat cow), they did not remove the animal to their own subterranean abodes, leaving no trace above ground; but the cow, to all appearance, was still in the possession of its owner, pining away under some unknown disease, and was said to be "elf-shot."

A crofter in a certain parish had a cow supposed to be "hurt frae dà grund," and an old woman called Maron o' Nort'-a-Voe —a famous witch doctor—was sent for.

On arriving at the house, Maron sent the goodman to the seashore to procure three crabs, of a kind called *cra's lupiks*. Meanwhile Maron provided herself with a *puttik* of tar, a steel *noraleg*, a leaf from a Bible, and a *lowin taand*. Thus equipped, she enters the byre. The cow is resting on the *bizzie*, unable to rise or eat.

Waving the fire-brand, she marches round the cow three times, against the sun, giving the beast a severe stab at each turn with the needle. The poor animal now jumps to its feet, while Maron proceeds to wave the leaf of holy writ over its back, at the same time muttering certain inaudible words in Norse. The fire-brand is placed in the tar pot and set at the cow's head, the smoke or *sneuker* of which excites a fit of coughing on the trembling animal. A cat is now brought on the scene, and set on the cow's neck, and dragged by the tail three times over the cow's back. Presently the old man arrives with the fairy crabs, and these are given in one dose all alive and kicking. Maron has now done her duty; the cow is delivered from the power of the *trows*. She leaves instructions that the ashes of the *taand* and the tar that remain in the pot be made into three pills, and these are to be given to the cow *blöd fastin* on three mornings.

The writer can remember a woman who claimed to have been taken by the *trows*, but who was mercifully delivered from their power by the skill of a famous witch-doctor.

It happened in this wise. When the woman, whose name was Meg, was nine months old, her mother left the child asleep in the cradle, and went into the byre to milk a cow. While thus engaged, she heard the child utter a terrible scream, and rushing into the house she found the bairn struggling and crying in a most excited manner. In vain she tried to soothe the child, in vain she sang sweet lullaby. Poor Meg cries and will not be comforted. She gets blue in the face and hoarse in the throat, and ·altogether so changed that even the mother cannot recognise her once thriving child. At last an old woman is brought to the house, and she declares that the bairn is "hurted frae da grund."

A bucket of salt water is fetched out of the breaking sea, and three small *ebb-stanes*. A large fire is put on the hearth and the stones are placed in it. The sea water is poured into the meat kettle, and the stones when red hot are thrown into it. Meg is stripped and placed in this bath. She is turned round in the kettle, three times with the sun and thrice in the opposite direction.

The child is now placed on a wet blanket, and passed through the flame of the peat fire three times. She is then swathed in this sheet and put to bed, after which she is burned in effigy. The mother is ·further instructed to "tig the nine mothers' maet" for the bairn's restoration—*i.e.*, nine mothers whose first born were sons are each solicited for an offering of three articles of food, to be used during the convalescence of the patient who has been thus snatched from the power of the *trows*. Meg lived to a good old age, and often related the story of her recovery to the writer.

The Wart o' Cleat in Whalsay was inhabited by *trows*, and many fair damsels were lured to this fairy abode, where they lived and brought forth children, who were changed into a sort of semi-spiritual existence. Consequently the service of skilled women of the daughters of men was in frequent demand.

Once it happened that the *trows* of Cleat sent a messenger to the mainland to fetch a *howdie* who dwelt in Lunna Ness; but the woman delayed to cross the Sound owing to the raging of the sea. At last, however, she consented to follow her guide, and setting out, bearing two kits of *faavers* (dainty meats) for the patient, they reached the eastern side of the Ness. Here they were met by another messenger from trowland, come to hasten their journey; but when the woman caught sight of the angry sea, she stood hesitating to cross. This conduct so exasperated the *trows* that they transformed her and the two kits into stone. The three stones stand there to this day as a warning to others who should hesitate to obey the *trows*.

Now, from the following legend it would appear that such fears were unnecessary. There lived in Fraam Gord a woman called Catherine Tammasdaughter, who practised midwifery. One dark, stormy night, as she and her husband were asleep, a messenger from the *trows* appeared at the bedside. Instead of the goodman getting up and having a say in the matter, he is thrown by a magic spell into the most profound slumber, so that he is quite oblivious to his wife's departure.

Catherine is soon ready, and is conducted to the seashore, where a small boat is in waiting. The night is dark and murky, and the sea is breaking on the shore, but fearlessly she takes her seat in the tiny skiff. With amazing speed they skim the waves, and soon she is landed in the Wick o' Gröten, in the island of Fetlar. Presently she is ushered into a spacious cavern, where a great company of strange beings are gathered together. The special object of Catherine's visit is soon accomplished, and she is presented with a tiny *pig* (jar), containing an oint-ment for anointing the new-born child. While she is performing this delicate operation, she accidentally touches one of her eyes. No sooner does the mysterious ointment touch the eyelid than she beholds a certain woman of her former acquaint-ance, who had been some time dead. Calling her by name, she exclaims: "Lass, what w'y is du come here?" "What e'e saw du yon wi'?" enquires one of the *trows*. "Dis ene," replies Catherine, pointing to her left eye. Immediately by an *elf-shot* she is struck blind on the eye that had been thus mysteriously opened to behold the secrets of this enchanted dwelling.

It is said that the *trows* were great lovers of music, and the fiddlers of the olden time could discuss lightsome lilts, known as "fairy reels," that had been learned from the *hillfolk*. A noted fiddler named John Herculeson had been invited to a wedding at Whiteness, where he was supposed to arrive early on the bridal e'en. The company waited long and patiently, but John did not turn up, and it was only on the eve of the "sindering day" that he reached the festive dwelling. Now, it turned out that John, while crossing the Hill of Wormidale, had been taken into a *trowie* abode, and had been kept playing the fiddle for two whole days. It was deemed imprudent to accept any reward from the *trows*, or to partake of their food.

I was told by an old man of my early acquaintance that on one occasion he was crossing Valafell in the gloaming of an autumn day, and being weary, he sat down to rest at the foot of Gulla Hammar. Not a breath of wind stirred the air; nor sound was heard, save the murmuring of the gentle waves that laved the adjacent shore. Presently he heard the strains of sweet music vibrating among the crevices of the rocks overhead. So distinct and continuous were the sounds that he learned the piece by ear, and subsequently taught it to a fiddler, who classed it among his best dance music, under the name of "The Trowie Reel."

A few legends of the fabled race of giants have come down to us. These stories are usually connected with the standing stones, or remarkable rocks or boulders.

A story is told of two giants called Herman and Saxe, who once lived in Unst. The former resided in a capacious *helyer* (cave) in the neighbourhood of Hermaness, called Herman's Ha', while

Saxe occupied a subterranean cavern in the side of the Muckle Pobie, called Saxe's Ha' to this day. Now, it happened that Herman had captured a whale at Burra-firth, and as it was exceptionally large, he asked neighbour Saxe for the loan of his kettle (a great, cauldron-shaped cavity in the rocks), in which to boil his gigantic prey. But Saxe, having an eye to business, would only lend the kettle on condition that he got half of the whale. These terms seemed exorbitant to Herman, and indignant at the churlish conduct of his neighbour, he seized a huge boulder and hurled it at Saxe. But, unlike the giant of Rönies Hill, he overshot the mark, and the stone fell into the sea near the Horns o' Haggmark, where it stands high above the waves, and bears the name of Herman's Stack.

A standing stone once stood near the old churchyard of Norwick, in Unst, which was also connected with the giant of the kettle. This stone had a hole in it, and its origin was traditionally said to be as follows. The giant Saxe came to Kirkatoon, where dwelt a famous *howdie* (midwife), whose services were required at his residence, and not finding a suitable fastening for the beast that he had brought to carry the *cummer*, he drove the monolith into the ground and pushed his thumb through it, making a hole, into which he tied his horse's rein.

About the beginning of the century doctors were few and far between, and the professional V.S. altogether unknown. Although our forefathers enjoyed a greater immunity from disease than we, whose constitutions are weakened by a foreign dietry, yet then, as now, both man and beast were liable to disease, the true nature of which was a mystery to our forefathers. In every parish there were persons who claimed to be possessed of the power to treat the sick. Most forms of illness were supposed to be either an "evil onwaar," or "hurted frae da grund." The former was the result of the evil prayer or wish of some wicked person skilled in the black art, the latter was the supernatural influence of *trows* or *hillfolk.* When a person fell sick, some skilful neighbour was at once called in and the person carefully examined.

If there was any tendency to shortness of breathing, the patient was asked to "pick the mills." This was done by repeating the following without drawing breath :

"Four-and-twenty millstanes hang upon a waa,
He was a good picker that picked them aa :

Picked ene,	Picked thirteen,
Picked twa,	Picked fourteen,
Picked tree,	Picked fifteen,
Picked four,	Picked sixteen,
Picked five,	Picked seventeen,
Picked six,	Picked eighteen,
Picked seven,	Picked nineteen,
Picked eight,	Picked twenty,
Picked nine,	Picked twenty-one,
Picked ten,	Picked twenty-two,
Picked 'leven,	Picked twenty-three,
Picked twal,	Picked twenty-four."

If the patient could pick eighteen to

twenty-four mills, the breathing or lungs were supposed to be in a fairly good condition, but if the sufferer further complained of having "lost dir stamack" (appetite), they were supposed to be afflicted with the "heart wear."

This disease assumed two forms, viz., the *aaber* and the *feckless*. In the former the heart was understood to be too big, and there was a voracious (*aaber*—greedy) appetite, without doing the body any good. In the latter—or *feckless* form—the heart was supposed to be wasting away under some *trowie* influence, and there was no desire for food. "Castin' or rinnin' da heart" and "tiggin' da nine women's maet" were the chief applications for these complaints.

The "castin' o' da heart" was performed as follows. A small quantity of lead was melted in a *kollie*, and the patient was set in the meat kettle before the fire. On the head was placed a blind sieve, in the centre of which a bowl of water was set. A pair of steel scissors or two keys were held in the hand of the operator in the form of a cross, and through the *bool* of the scissors or key the molten lead was poured into the water. The numerous shapes assumed by the lead were carefully examined, and the operation was repeated until a piece was found in form like the human heart. This was sewn in the left breast of some article of underclothing and worn by the patient for three moons. Further, the water used in this ceremony was made into porridge, of which the patient partook seated in the "guit o' da door," at the hour of sunset. In casting the heart, attention was paid to the moon : for the *aaber* heart-wear the time chosen was the waning moon and the ebbing tide, and for the *feckless* form the opposite was deemed the most fitting time.

The most serious forms of disease were "mort-caald" and "inbred fever," which no doubt corresponds with our bronchitis and influenza. *Gulsa*, or the yellow disease (jaundice), was treated by an oil obtained from the *gulsa whelk*, or garden snail.

In sprained joints the *wrestin treed* was considered the best remedy. This thread was made of black wool, and knotted in a peculiar way, viz., a knot for every day in the moon's age. This was tied round the sprained joint, the operator muttering in an undertone :

> " Da Loard raed,
> Da foal slaed,
> Sinnin ta sinnin,
> Bane ta bane,
> Hael i' da Father,
> Da Son, an' da
> Holy Ghost's name."

Burning and toothache were " told out " by uttering over the patient certain formulas of words in Norse, only known to the speaker. Ringworm was " told out " in a rather peculiar way. The practitioner took three straws, on each of which were three knots or joints, and lighting these in the fire, the following

words were uttered while the straws
burned :

> "Ringwirm, ringwirm, red,
> Saand be dy maet
> An' fire be dy bed ;
> Aye may du dwine,
> An' never may du spread."

Then the part affected was dusted over
with the ashes of the burned straws, and
the unburned parts were deposited under
a *mör fael*.

For sprains and bruises, and affections
of an inflammatory nature, a form of cupping called *horn blöd* was very frequently
employed, and even yet is not quite obsolete ; and I am of opinion that no more
effectual mode of cupping or local bleeding
can be practised.

The *blöd-horn* was commonly made of
the horn of a quey or young cow. It was
about four inches long, and from an inch
and a half to two inches in diameter at the
wide end. The horn was scraped and
dressed, the small end being perforated

and wrapped round with a bit of dried bladder. The operator sucked the horn to the affected part, thus making a circle on the skin. The spot thus marked was *saxed* or scarified so as to bleed. The horn was now applied, the contained air being extracted by sucking with the mouth. The pressure of the external air caused the folds of the bladder to shut the perforation of the horn, and thus prevented the ingress of air from without. In order to accelerate the flow of blood and reduce the local inflammation, a warm fomentation was applied round the base of the horn. *Howdies* generally possessed *blöd-horns*, and were the chief practitioners.

Recourse was often had to certain waters that were supposed to possess healing virtues. Helga Water, in North-mavine, and Yelabrön or Hielyaburn, in the island of Unst, were famous for their health-giving properties, as the names seem to imply. The latter is one of the finest springs in the island, flowing with undiminished abundance during the most prolonged drought of summer, bubbling up from a gravelly bed as clear as crystal. Regarding this spring the story is told of a certain priest who came to teach the old inhabitants the doctrine of the "White Christ." But such was their attachment to the ancient religion, that they not only refused to hear this messenger, but conspired to put him to death. Consequently, as he journeyed near the Heugins o' Watley, he was waylaid and seized by a band of rude barbarians. Seeing that his end was come, he craved a few moments' respite for prayer. This being granted, the priest kneeled down and prayed that since the people would not hear his doctrine for the benefit of their souls, there might a fountain flow from his grave for the healing of their bodies. Here the good man was killed, and here on the solitary hillside he was buried; but from his grave their burst forth in perennial flow the healing fountain of Yelabrön.

All persons taking water from this spring brought an offering of three stones, or it might be three coins. Hence at the head of the spring a large cairn of stones has been collected, and I remember when a boy finding old Danish coins there.

When water was brought from this well for sick folk, the journey was made between the hours of sunset and sunrise, and generally the person that bore the medicinal water obtained an inkling of the patient's chance to recover. It might be they heard a *gaenfore* or saw a *feyness*; a white mouse or a black fowl might cross their path. Water from this well must not touch the ground; hence the vessel containing it was generally set on the top of a millstone or *knockin' stane.*

A person likely to die was said to be *fey*, and a *gaenfore* or *feyness* was a prelude of death. Numerous things—both sights and sounds—were said to forebode death in a house or neighbourhood. For example, a cock crowing at an unseasonable hour of the night, the seeing of an owl or a corncrake, a rainbow having both its ends inside a "toon dyke," were all looked upon as evil omens.

Hearing certain sounds in old wood, called a *shaek*, foreboded important events. These sounds are doubtless produced by tiny insects in the wood, but our superstitious forefathers heard them as the voice of Fate. A sound like the ticking of a watch was called a "marriage shaek," a vibrating sound a "flitting shaek," and a dropping sound a "dead shaek."

The following names were applied to diseases of animals :—

Turkasöt—The skin adhering firmly to the back.
Lungasöt—Form of bronchitis.
Whirkabis or *Bulga*—Dropsical swelling in the throat.
Sturdie—Water on the brain.
Yogar or *Spaegie*—Rheumatic affections of the joints.
Sköl—A mouth disease in horses.
Gaaners—A mouth disease in cows.
Feerie—An epidemic disease among dogs.

For all these maladies some antidote was found, and may have proved as effectual as some of the modern concoctions of the now-a-days V.S.

The skilful housewife could diagnose her cow's ailments by carefully noting the various tones of sound uttered by the animal in health and disease. The following names were applied to sounds made by a cow :—

> *Bröl*—The ordinary, natural sound.
> *Gul-bröl*—An emphatic or excited *bröl*.
> *Skröl*—A frightened sound.
> *Umble*—A throat sound, as if choking.
> *Njoag*—A nasal sound.
> *Drund*—A moaning sound.

Sounds made by other animals were :

> *Sneg* and *Nikker*—By horses.
> *Eer*, *Reein*, and *Loadie-grunt*—By the pig.
> *Nyrr*—By the cat.
> *Peester*—By the mouse.
> *Klaug*—By the hen.
> *Oob*—By the seal.
> *Yarm*—By the sheep.

There were several superstitious notions

connected with the cock. It was exceedingly lucky to possess a black cock. There was a belief that *trows* were quite powerless within sound of its crowing. "A black cock with a red breast had more virtue than a priest."

Women at the time of child-bearing were especially liable to be taken by the *hillfolk*, and hence the midwife was generally an expert in the art of preserving her charge from the *trows*. When a birth was about to take place, it was customary to borrow a black cock to have in the house. The ordinary rooster did not trouble himself to crow save at midnight and in the morning, but the swart bird of which we speak detected the *vaam* of any unseen presence, and announced the same by crowing at any hour. When a cock was heard crowing at an unseasonable time, it was understood that some *fey* person (doomed to die) was within hearing ; and if a person had met with any serious fright, the living heart was torn from the breast of the cock, and applied bleeding to the left breast of the individual affected.

The *trows* sometimes , rendered themselves visible to ordinary mortals, and are said to have left behind them some of their own domestic utensils, the possession of which was reckoned very lucky.

In a house near a place called Gungsta a wooden cog was captured from a *trowie* wife, and this cog or kit was possessed for generations, and used for milking; and whether the cow was *teed*, *forrow*, or *yield*, the cog was filled to the brim. A cow in full milk is said to be *teed*; in second year's milk, without having a calf, *forrow*; having no milk, *yield*.

A similar vessel, said to have been obtained from the *trows*, was long preserved in the North Isles as a *maet-löm* for any animal supposed to be suffering from the evil eye.

The following legend is told regarding it. A certain goodwife had risen about *da swaar o' simmer dim* to get a little milk for her child. As she entered the byre, she beheld a *trow* milking her cow. She stood spell-bound, unable to speak or move. Presently the. *trowie* wife exclaimed :

> " Himpie, hornie, hoy,
> Minnie kum carl mi mug."

Or according to another version :

> " O, when an' döl, da bairn is faaen
> I' da fire an' brunt."

The woman now had power to "sain hersel'," and the *trow* went like lightning out the byre *lum*, dropping the kit as she went.

An old man named Henry Farquhar or Forker is asleep on a bench in the corner of the *butt-end*. In the small hours of the morning he is awakened by the glimmer of a weird light. He sees a *trow* enter carrying a new-born child. In her hand she holds a tiny jar of peculiar workmanship. He tries to "sain himsel'," but is powerless. But on the *bauk* sit two cocks, the one white and the other black. As this strange visitor proceeds to anoint her child with the contents of the jar, the white cock crows, and the *trow* says :

> " The white cock is nae cock,
> Waadie, Waadie,
> I can sit still an' warm me baby."

But presently the black cock crows, and, jumping up, the *trow* exclaims :

> " The black cock is a cock,
> Waadie, Waadie,
> I maun noo flit frae warmin' me baby."

The spell that bound old Farquhar is broken, and, jumping up from his couch, he seizes the jar on the hearthstone. Hence the origin of " Forker's Pig."

This *pig* or jar was made of unglazed clay, holding about a gill. It was preserved with great care, and was fetched here and there to persons supposed to be hurt by *trows*. The last possessor of the said *pig* gave it to the writer several years ago.

SOCIAL LIFE IN OLDEN TIMES.

The young folks of the present generation have little idea of the way in which our forefathers lived. The luxuries and conveniences to which we are accustomed were then unknown. The inhabitants of these islands subsisted almost entirely on their native productions. The harvest of the land, eked out by the harvest of the sea, furnished their sole means of subsistence; and it is no matter for surprise to hear old people speaking of the "scarce years."

Stories have been handed down of the seasons of want and the extreme shifts to which the people were sometimes reduced. Near the sites of old townships enormous quantities of shells, particularly whelks, may be dug up, showing that these have been extensively used as food.

Their supplies were drawn from the crops of oats, bere, potatoes, and cabbage; from the sheep that lived in the scattalds;

and from the fish that swarmed round the shores. It may be said that these still form the staple means of support. True, but we do not use them as our fathers did. We barter them for tea from China and Ceylon, for sugar from the West Indies, for flour ground in Canadian mills, and for fruits and condiments from the shores and islands of the Mediterranean. We do not clothe ourselves with the warm fleece of the sheep, but exchange it for flimsy fabrics from the mills of Manchester, printed calicoes, and bright metal trinkets.

On a Shetland croft of last century the dwelling-house, barn, and byre were built together, so that access could be had to all parts from within. Ingress to and egress from the dwelling was commonly through the byre. When this was not the case, the door was protected by a *töfa*, or porch. The barn was furnished with a kiln for drying corn, built in a corner, and about six feet long by three broad. A few thin lathes, called " kiln trees," lay from side to side. These were covered with a thin layer of *gloy* (straw), on which the corn was spread. The fire burned under the *chylpin-stane* in the kiln *huggie*, and needed

FIG. 11.—*Shetland Hand-Mill.*

constant watching. At the side of the kiln stood a large straw basket, called a *skeb*, in which the corn was rubbed by foot when dried. On the wall hung a straw mat, called a *flakkie*, on which the corn was winnowed after being thrashed, and to separate the *dumba* before being ground. In the barn also was the hand-mill (Fig. 11), resting on a rude table called a *looder*. This mill was and still is chiefly used for grinding *burstin* (corn dried in a kettle over the fire). Well-made bere *burstin* makes delicious bread.

In the corner of the *butt-end* lay the *knockin' stane* and *mell*, for the purpose of shelling bere, or barley, as a delicacy for *helly* days and Sunday dinners. At the burn close by stood the water-mill (Fig. 12), on which the crop was ground during the *yarrowin*. The mill was driven by a rude, horizontal water-wheel, called a *tirl*. Over the "eye" of the mill was suspended an apparatus through which the corn passed, consisting of a *happer*, *shö*, and *klapper*. In a corner of the *looder* stood a *toyeg* (a small straw basket), containing as much corn as would be a *hurd o'*

FIG. 12.—*Shetland Water-Mill.*

burstin. This was the annual offering to the Water Neugle, in order to insure the good services of his godship. When this was neglected, the Neugle would sometimes grasp the *tirl* and stop the mill, and could only be dislodged by dropping a firebrand down by the *lightnin' tree.* The ground meal was sifted in sieves made of sheep-skin, fastened tightly round a hoop or rim, and perforated with red-hot *reva-twirries* (straightened out fish hooks). When sifted, the meal fell into three divisions—meal, groats, and *ootsiftins*, from the last of which that delicious food called *sooans*, and that healthy tonic beverage known as *swats*, are made.

In the yard near the *stiggie* was often to be seen a small *skroo* of corn, standing apart from the rest. This was the annual offering set apart to Broonie, a household deity whose good services were thus secured, particularly in protecting the corn yard and thatch roofs during the storms of winter. No article of clothing was ever devoted to this imaginary being, for—

> " When Broonie got a cloak or hood,
> He did his master nae mair good."

One of the most interesting appendages of the croft was the sheep *krö*. Here lads and lasses met to *roo* the sheep and mark the lambs, and sometimes in scarce years to *kavel* the lambs. The *krö* is a small round enclosure into which sheep are driven, and to facilitate the driving small branch dykes run out in two directions from the *krö*. These were termed *soadin* or *rexter* dykes, and sometimes *steugies*. In the *krö* the uniformity of colour observable in other flocks is wanting. Here is a blending of numerous shades, black, white, brown, and grey being the most common, while there is a sprinkling of *blyeag* (dirty white), *shaela* (steel gray), *moorit* (the colour of brown peat), and *catmuggit* (having the belly of a different colour). Everyone knew his own sheep by the marks cut in their ears. No two persons could have the same mark. If anyone got a lamb from another, an *oobregd* (off-break) mark must be put thereon. The various sheep marks had names by which they were known, *bits*, *crooks*, *fidders*, and *shöls* indicating different cuts in the ear. The people were constantly among the hills tending their sheep and *kyndin* the cows; and there was scarcely a spot that was not called by some appropriate name of Norse origin, such beautiful characteristic names as *Grunna Blaet* (the green spot), *Swarta Blaet* (the black or dark spot), *Gulla Hammar* (the yellow rocks), *Rora Klaet* (the red rocks). Many others might be named. Animals too had names, generally derived from their colour, such as *Sholma* (white face), *Sponga* (spotted), *Greema* (white spotted on the cheeks), *Rigga* (having a stripe running along the back), *Cullya* (polled), etc. These names all end in *a*, and denote the feminine gender. The masculine of animal names ended in *i* or *e*.

Since there was little or no imported grain, meal was a scarce commodity, and had to be most economically used, whether baked into *brönies*, *bannocks*, or *kröls*. Cabbage entered largely into the winter dietary, in such preparations as *lang kale*, *short kale*, and *tartanpurry*. Tea was almost unknown. The *blaandie-kaulik* and the *swatsi-swaarik* did duty instead of the golden tips of Ceylon. But fish was the chief article of food. Every house almost had a *skjo* (open built hut for drying fish), in which fish was stored for future use. Fish for home consumption was seldom salted, but preserved in various ways, such as *reested* (dried inside with fire and smoke), *blawn* (dried in the wind), and *gozened* (dried in the sun).

The liver of the fish was extensively used in a fresh state, and entered into the formation of numerous nutritious dishes, such as *stap*, *gree'd fish*, *liver heads*, *liver muggies*, *krampies*, *krappin*, *mooguildin*, *hakka muggies*, and *slot*. To this extensive use of fish livers may be attributed the hardihood of the old Shetlander, and the almost perfect immunity from some fatal forms of disease that afflict us in these days. One cannot but feel sad to see some poor, diseased form of humanity advised as a last resource to "try cod liver oil." Had the dietary afore-mentioned been attended to, the disease calling for fish oil treatment would probably never have been engendered.

But, alas, our inshore handline fishing is a thing of the past. The trawlers are killing the goose that laid the golden egg.

A WHALSAY MAN'S SOLILOQUY.

"O, for da days whan codlins wis rife,
 Whan stap an' gree'd fish wis da joy o' mi life,
 Whan frae moarnin' ta e'enin' on da sheek o' a
   gjo
 Ye could ha' pokket or drawn da fill o' a skjo.
 Dan a' kinds o' sma' fish adoarned da raeps,
 An' piltik an' sillok lay soornin' in haeps;
 Dere wis kippoks o' haddocks an' weel-speeted
   hoes;
 Heads dow'd, vam'd an draven, affectin' da nose;

Dere wis langies o' turbot 'at hang i' da reest,
An' hoe eggs resemblin' a truncher o' beest;
An' beautiful muggies, spleetin' wi gree,
Da bite o' your teeth sent a spoot i' your e'e.
Dat wis da stuff for greasin' your t'roat,
Or aetin' benon a kettle o' slot!
If a body haed risen ta look at da watch,
Ta spit i' da fire wis as guid as a match.
Baith aald folk an' young folk, frae Sodom ta
    Clate,
Spent da lang winter night in rivin' hard skate.
If it is ordeen'd I never sall see
Da chauds an' da krampies, da oceans o' gree,
Dis I can say—I'll remember forever
Da blessin' 'at cam frae da fish an' its liver."

Let us now return to the crofter's house. It is night, and the old man has returned from the handline fishing. His *böddie* is well stocked with fish. He sits by the round fire, with a *baet o' gloy* or a *kirvie o' floss*, winding it may be *simmonds* or *gurdastöries* for his *maeshies* and *riva-kessies*. In the corner in past the fire, (which was on the middle of the floor), on the *lit-kettle*, sits an old grandmother or a " quarter wife " rocking the cradle, or holding in her lap a *ramished* bairn, which she soothes by singing :

> " Husha baa baet dee,
> Minnie is gaen ta saet dee,
> Fur ta pluck an' fur ta pu',
> An' fur ta gadder luckies' oo,
> Fur ta buy a bull's skin
> Ta row peerie weerie in."

Or, it may be, in more dolorous tones she sings :

> " Husha baa, Minnie's daaty,
> We sall pit da trows awa';
> Broonie sinna git da bairn,
> If he comes da cocks 'ill craw."

If the fractious child has been silenced by the mention of Broonie, it will be dandled with lightsome lilt as granny sings :

> " Upride, upride, upride da bairn ;
> Ride awa, ride awa, ride awa da Neugle ;
> Haud dee tongue, cuddle doon,
> An' du sall git a buggle.

No person is idle. The grown-up females of the household are busily engaged preparing wool for the loom, which is to be made into underclothing for the family, or dyed with *blue-lit, old man skrottie, korkalit*, or *yellowin' girs*, as suiting to the goodman of the house or dresses for the females.

Perhaps some neighbour lad has called to "hadd him oot o' langour," to hear the old man's *klak* news, or what is ·more likely, to spend the evening in sweet companionship with the oldest lass. The common pastime for such occasions was "layin' up guddiks," *i.e.*, propounding riddles. The simple pastimes were of native origin, but considerable ingenuity was shown in weaving out of the scant material at hand a programme for an evening's entertainment.

I shall here record a few *guddiks* (riddles) and other fireside amusements that were used by our forefathers in their social gatherings, to while away the long winter evenings. I believe the only specimen of the kind now extant, and of Norse origin, is that mentioned in Dr. Jacobsen's "Shetland Dialect." I remember hearing it in Norwick, Unst, about forty years ago, but I had quite forgotten it until it was reproduced in the valuable work referred to. It is as follows:

> "Fira hunga, fira gunga,
> Fira staad ipo skö,
> Twa veestra vaig a bee,
> An' een comes atta driljandie."

This riddle, as explained by Dr. Jacobsen, has reference to the cow, viz.:

> "Four hanging—the teats,
> Four going—the legs,
> Four standing upwards—horns and ears,
> And one comes behind shaking—the tail."

I have heard in several parts of Shetland what appears to be an Anglicised variant of the same:

> "Four hingers and four gangers,
> Twa luckers and twa crookers,
> Twa laavers and ae dillie-daunder."

Again, here is another riddle, the meaning of which is a woman milking a cow:

> "Tink-tank, twa in a bank,
> Ten about four."

> " I grew wi' da coo, yet was made by a man,
>   I böre till his moo what boiled i' da pan."

The meaning of this is a horn spoon. In olden times these were of native manufacture. They were often termed *gaeppies* on account of their size, which required the mouth to be widely opened.

> " I ha'e three feet, bit not ae haand ;
>   I ha'e five maids at my commaand ;
>   I ha'e ae e'e, bit canna see ;
>   I ha'e twa haerts in my bodie ;
>   I go fu' faster than a mill,
>   An' yet my feet are staandin' still ;
>   An' whether I am in or oot,
>   My guts are always me withoot."

This is a perfect description of a Shetland spinning wheel. The "guts" referred to the wheel-band, which was made of the intestines of sheep, and was called *term*.

> " Four-neukit, tail-teukit,
>   An' teeth oot o' number."
>
> *Answer*—Wool cards.

> " What is it 'at tears een anidder a' day,
>   An' sleeps in een anidder's airms a' nicht."
>
> *Answer*—Wool cards.

" What is it that goes through a rock, through a
  reel, through an aald spinny wheel, through
  a sheep's shank bane."

Answer—A web of cloth.

" I gaed atween twa wids,
  An' I cam' atween twa watters."

Answer—One going to the well with
wooden buckets.

" Peerie fool (fowl) featherless,
  New come oot o' Paradise,
  Fleein' ower da mill dam,
  Catch me if du be a man."

Answer—A snowflake.

" Hookatee, krookatee, foo rins du?
  Clipped tail every year, why spör's du?"

This is what the meadow and the brook
said to each other.

" Roond like a millstane,
  Lugged like a cat,
  Staandin' upo' three legs—
  Can du guess dat?"

Answer—A kettle.

" Twa grey grumphies lay in ae sty,
  Da maer dey get, da maer dey cry;
  Da less dey get, da stiller dey lie."

Answer—The millstones.

> " I gaed oot ae moarnin' in May,
>   I fan a thing in a cole o' hay,
>   It wis nedder fish, flesh, feather, or bane,
>   Bit I kept it till it could gaeng its lane."
>
> *Answer*—An egg.

These may serve as specimens of Shetland riddles. There was scarcely anything either about the house, within or without the house, that was not made the subject of a *guddik*.

Another favourite pastime was *going in wads* (forfeits). There were various forms practised in this game. I shall mention one that I remember seeing in Unst, and which, I doubt not, is very old.

The young people are seated round the open fireplace. A piece of straw, or better still, of dried dockweed, say about eight inches long, is bent in the form of an acute triangle. Both the ends are lighted in the fire and begin to burn slowly, something like a cigar. It is now carefully balanced at the angular point on another straw held perpendicularly in the hand of No. 1, who exclaims : " Wha'll buy my jantle Jockie belaand ? " No. 2 answers : " What if he dees i' dy ain haand ? " No. 2 replies : " Da back sall bear da saddle baand, thro' moss, thro' mire, thro' mony a laand, that gars my jantle Jockie dee or get a faa." The burning triangle is now handed to No. 2, who repeats the same formula together with No. 3, and so on to the next; and anyone in whose hand the " gentle Jockie dees " (fire goes out) or " gets a faa " (falls) that one is in a *wad*, and is punished (?) by kissing every person of the opposite sex present, or by answering a number of dark questions, commonly having reference to love and courtship.

Straw was put to numerous uses by the old Shetlander. It was food and bedding for his cattle. It thatched his roof and formed his couch at night. The very seat on which he sat was made of this humble material. It furnished another favourite subject for evening amusement. No. 1 of the party begins by asking No. 2 : " What öse is strae for?" No. 2 replies: "Strae is for mony a guid öse, particularly ta mak' saat cuddies (small baskets for salt) o'. What öse is strae for?" No. 3 answers: "Strae is for mony a good öse, if it wis bit ta mak' a wizzie o'. What öse is strae for?" And so on, round and round, until someone at last failed to find a use for straw that had not been previously mentioned.

SHETLAND FESTIVITIES.

We who live in these days have our social gatherings, our picnics and soirees, our balls and club meetings, etc. These names were unknown to our forefathers. Yet we learn that they were a highly social people. It was in their nature to rejoice with them that rejoiced and to weep with them that wept. The fishermen tarried for one another, and the husbandman did not consider his own work completed until his neighbour's crop was in the yard. They had not acquired

that selfishness which is an outgrowth of
our so-called modern civilisation whose
policy is: "Man mind dysel', an deil tak'
the hinmost." The *upstaander* and the
yarmer had not then learned to quarrel
over a "mug o' lū watter."

In the festivities of the olden time there
seems to have been special respect paid to
the number three. For example, during
the season the crew of a *haf* boat had
three feasts, viz.: the *Doon-drawin'* at
Beltane; the *Johnsmas* at Midsummer,
when they supped the "milgruel kits";
and the *Foy* at Lammas, when the fishing
closed.

When births, marriages, and deaths
occurred, there were three feasts in connection with each. On the occasion of a
birth there was the *Blithe-feast*, when the
child was born; the *Fittin'-feast*, when the
mother came to the fire and resumed her
duties; and the *Christenin'*, when the child
was baptised. In connection with a marriage there were the *Spörin'*, the *Contract*,

and the *Bridal*, which commonly "stood" three days. *Spör* means to ask or enquire—hence the *spörin'* was the occasion when the bridegroom asked in a formal way the consent of the bride's parents. Even at the final and most solemn event of life the three feasts were still observed, viz,, the *Kistin'*, the *Funeral*, and the *Condolin'*.

Winter was the chief season of festivity. As a rule all marriages took place during the three winter moons.

Arrangements were made about the beginning of November for holding the Hallowmas banquets. The young lads banded themselves together in squads and went *hoosamylla* (from house to house), as maskers, commonly called *gröliks*. They received offerings of money, *burstin brönies*, legs of *vivda*, or dried *sparls*. When the rounds of the district had been completed, they repaired to a neighbouring barn with their sweethearts, and the banquet was spread. They amused themselves with such games as *hunt-da-slipper*, *wads*, and *haand-de-kroopin.* The singing of good old ballads and the "laying up" of *guddiks* gave variety to the entertainment. But more frequently these guileless maidens and their happy lovers tripped with lightsome lilt the old Shetland reels, such as "Nippin' Grund," "Da Brunt Scones o' Voe," "Da Scalloway Lasses," "Shak'-'im-troose," "Kale an' Knocked Corn," etc.

There is a desire in the human mind to pry into the future, and even at the present day, in this land of Kirks and Bibles, you may see jolly lads in H.M. uniform and braw young lasses patronising the professional cup and card reader. The chief object of the Hallowmas sports of the olden time was to get a peep on the other side of the curtain that separates the present from the future. I shall relate a few of the old customs practised at the Hallowmas festival.

Drappin' Glasses.—This was performed by dropping a small portion of the white of an egg into a glass of water. The forms assumed prognosticated the future in matters of love, fortune, and death.

Tyin' the Kale Stock.—For this purpose the young folks went blindfold into the kale-yard, and each one tied his or her garter round the first kale-stock they touched, and the number of shoots on the *kastik*, which was counted in the morning, was a forecast of the family of the future.

Castin' the Clew.—This was a more elaborate affair, and required a consider-able amount of nerve for its performance. At the dead of night one person alone went to the water-mill, and getting on the roof, dropped a ball of worsted in through the *lum*, holding fast the end. Then the operator on the roof began to rewind the clew into another ball, repeating the while in a steady tone: " Wha hadds my clew end?" Then a voice from out the dark mill was expected to answer the name of the future husband or wife.

Turnin' the Sleeve.—This was performed at the hour of midnight. A person wishing to read the future by this means went all alone and unseen, and wet their shirt sleeve in a burn over which a corpse had been borne. They next retired to a barn or other outhouse and kindled a fire, hanging up the wet shirt as if to dry. The owner of the shirt now retires to the opposite end of the barn and lies down to wait. As the hours pass away, the dying embers cast weird shadows on the walls. Presently, amid the gloom and fitful flicker an apparition is seen flitting across the floor and silently turning the wet sleeve. This is none other than the phantom of the future husband or wife. If nothing is seen and the shirt remains unturned, the prier into futurity may look forward to a life of single bliss. But sometimes it was said that the dark outline of a coffin was seen, warning the poor watcher to prepare for another world.

Fathomin' the Skroo.—As has already

been stated, in olden times a small stack, commonly bere, was set apart as an annual offering to *Broonie*. Now, one went blindfold into the corn yard and fathomed this *skroo*, three times with the sun and thrice *widdershins*, and at the last turn they were supposed to clasp in their embrace the form of their lover—perhaps Broonie himself.

Siftin' Siller.—The operator in this case went alone into a room having a window, and placing a looking-glass opposite, he took his stand between the window and the mirror, having his back turned towards the window. Then, with three silver coins in a seive, he sifted away, steadfastly gazing at the mirror, in which, be it observed, a view reflected from the window was obtained. While this was going on, he expected to behold, passing before his astonished gaze in a sort of panoramic order, the whole of his future life.

Passin' the Harrow.—This was a performance seldom practised, except by some person of a "deil-may-care" disposition, for while the other Hallowmas sports had for their object merely the forecasting of matters matrimonial, this was supposed to unfold the future, even the spirit-world; and the person who had the hardihood to "go i' da harrow" never revealed what they either saw or heard, and always warned others not to try such a trick. The performance was very simple. Three harrows were placed, some distance apart, outside the open fodder door of an old barn, and at the hour of midnight a person went blindfold into the yard and passed back foremost over each harrow in turn, thence through the barn window, and at the end of this journey he was supposed to fall into a sort of trance and hear and see unutterable things.

When Hallowmas was past, the people set themselves in right earnest to their winter duties. Handline or *klak* fishing was practised when weather permitted, and the *skjos* were well stocked with fish for the approaching Yule festivities. During stormy weather the men were occupied in making numerous articles for domestic use from straw, such as *kessies, mael böddies, skebs, toyegs, flakkies, rivakessies, simmond-chairs, saat kuddies*, etc.

The women were occupied carding and spinning wool, although the manufacture of *wadmil* had long ceased. The making of cloth for home wear was universally practised, and in almost every township there could be found the professional *wobster* (weaver), whose busy shuttle seldom stopped the livelong winter. Here and there were persons of artistic skill whose business it was to *taat* bed rugs with wool dyed in *blue lit, skrottie, kurka-lit, aald man*, or *yellowin' girs*. The social disposition of the people led them to spend much of their time, especially the long winter evenings, in each other's houses, whiling away the time in telling stories of the sea, tales of adventures with *trows* and witches, stories of smugglers, wrecks, and press-gang, together with more rational affairs both general and domestic. No finer specimen of the home talk of the olden time can be given than is contained in "Shetland Fireside Tales," and the "Fireside Cracks" of the *Shetland Times*.

To the young and gay winter wore slowly away, and many a time and oft did old matrons answer the question, "Is it lang ta Yule?" At last the 20th of December (O.S.) dawns, and a look of joy and expectancy may be seen on every face. The "muckle wheel" is taken off the *butt* wall, and *cairds* and *knuck*s, *sweeries* and *reels*, are laid aside for a season. The handmill is taken off the *sile* and turned upside down on the *looder*, lest during the *helly days* it should be driven *widdershins* by witch and warlock. The Yule peats are carried in, and a *reested* cow's head or sheep's head is laid in steep for the Byaena-Sunday *brose*.

This is Tammasmas E'en, and the day following is Tammasmas Day, in which no manner of work can be done.

> " Ta shape or shu,
>   Ta bake or brew,
>   Ta reel a pirm
>   Or wind a clew,
>   A lö soolpaltie
>   Will tak you."

Even—

> " Da bairn i' da midder's wime
>   'Ill mak' woefu' döl,
>   If wark be wrought on Tammasmas night,
>   Five nights afore Yule."

At last Yule morning dawns. This is the chief festival of the season. At other times there may be scant, but now there is no want. It is true, everything is of native origin and simplicity, but still a wonderful variety may be seen. Every person, old and young, wears something new on Yule morning. The round peat fire blazes to the *crook-bauk*. The *kollie* (Fig. 13), well fed with *sillok* oil, hangs on the *raep*, illuminating the *butt-end*. The *ben* room is lighted with an irregular tallow dip, stuck in the neck of an empty Dutch " krook."

The day is spent in feasting, and at

FIG. 13.—*Shetland Kollie.*

night the service of the local fiddler is called for, and the merry-go-round of the Shetland *Rant* is kept up from house to house until Four-an'-twenty Day (18th January, O.S.), when the exhausted larders reminded the people that it was time to resume the more stern duties of life.

The last festival of winter was Fastern's E'en, a movable feast, about the beginning of February.

> " First comes Candlemas,
>   An' dan da new mön,
>   An' dan comes Fastern's E'en
>   Whin a' da guid is döne."

www.ingramcontent.com/pod-product-compliance
Lightning Source LLC
Chambersburg PA
CBHW021826090726
47818CB00077BA/62